A Ray of Sunshine

ALEXIA ST. PIERRE

WESTBOW
PRESS®
A DIVISION OF THOMAS NELSON
& ZONDERVAN

WestBow Press books may be ordered through booksellers or by contacting:

WestBow Press
A Division of Thomas Nelson & Zondervan
1663 Liberty Drive
Bloomington, IN 47403
www.westbowpress.com
1 (866) 928-1240

ISBN: 978-1-6642-0038-8 (sc)
ISBN: 978-1-6642-0039-5 (e)

Print information available on the last page.

WestBow Press rev. date: 08/19/2020

I DEDICATE THIS BOOK TO ...

*My amazing BIG Mexican family and all my friends that have
helped me every step of the way. But in specific my handsome,
loving husband Kaleb, my beautiful baby girls Hadassah and
Sadie Sophia. My strong and stunning mom Rosy alongside
with the best brother ever Andre'. I know it's long but it's
important to finish with my Mother-in-love Dorothy (who
helped me edit this book) and Father-in-love Patrick.*

*But most importantly to my Abba Daddy, JESUS
without you none of this would have been possible
and who knows where I would have been.*

I Love you ALL

Contents

CHAPTER 1

Leap of Faith

For many years, I have thought about writing my story but every time I would sit down and put my pen to the paper, either no words would come to me, or words of hate would just "blurb" all over the pages. How could I tell my story? Would anyone read it? Would it help? I never could write or express my words well, so it was easy to buy the lie. The lie that I was not able and to just give up on my testimony and on me. But that is not the case anymore because I know that if no one reads this or if only one person does, this is not about me. This is about my Abba Father, and this is about Jesus entrusting me to share my story and to wait no longer. As I take the leap of faith and start to write... the words are just coming!

When I sit back and reflect on my life, I realize that God has been with me since my first breath. For 17 years I did not know that. My life is no different than yours in the fact that we both have life, breath, eyes, hands etc. and that, most importantly, we were created by God. It is by no mistake that we are on this planet.

But there is a difference between each of us too in that we all have had a different journey. And that is what I want to talk to you about. My journey. My "not so pretty" journey, but a journey that does in fact, have a fairy tale ending.

Before I begin to share my story with you however, I want to give you a disclaimer. I will be talking about Jesus. But please don't stop reading if you don't believe in Jesus because I didn't believe in Him either! I knew about God because I had been raised with a Catholic background. It seems to just be something that you are born into if you are Mexican! We did the typical Christmas and Easter visits to church, but that was basically it. Here's the thing: It doesn't matter what journey you are, or are not on, with God - whether you have known Him all your life, just recently heard of Him, or don't want anything at all to do with Him. You may be wrestling with: *How can such a loving God allow so much hurt to happen in the world? Why did I have to suffer?* I know I blamed God for everything I felt. *How could such a good God "allow" my own father to sexually abuse me? Does He not see my pain and my tears? Can't He hear me?! And why didn't He protect me?*

I can tell you one thing: God did not abandon you. He did not abandon me. And it was never His plan for any hurt to happen to you or to me. No matter where you turn, He is the only way to fill you. You will NEVER find complete healing, peace, or joy without Him. Trust me. I know. How do I know? Well keep reading and find out!

There is one thing that I need you to understand before we begin. In this book, I will not be sharing all the gory details of my abuse, and I have a very specific reason for that. Hearing all the details of another person's story can cause an abused victim to compare their own story with the one they are reading about and comparing whether or not theirs was worse. So, if yours appears to be "less", you can tend to dismiss your abuse as not worthy of dealing with. If your own appears "more severe", the tendency is to become discouraged feeling that even this book cannot help you. What I need you to understand is that the issue is not about how severe your abuse was because ANY degree of abuse has the same spirit attached to it. No matter how "big" or "small" it was. Regardless of the degree of your abuse, this book has been written to help you come to healing and freedom. For it is the same guideline for all.

And so, I begin my story. Between the ages of three and sixteen, I was sexually abused by my father. With that comes all other kinds of other abuse too: mental, verbal, emotional and so forth. I tried to take my own life many times between the ages of seven and seventeen with three near fatal attempts. But this is just the introduction to what I will be talking about in this book. One thing this book is not about is self-pity or how horrible my life used to be. I am not here to dwell on the past, but I am going to share with you my experience and my transformation from a Victim to a Victor. I can confidently and boldly say that I am FREE! I am living an amazing life. I am happy. I am cleansed. I am healed. I am redeemed. I am forgiven. I am loved. I am a daughter to a perfect Father. And most importantly, I have learned not to dwell in the, "*WHY did this happen to me?*", but instead in the "*Oh! How much God loves me!*" I have chosen to forgive my father for all that he has done to me and my family, and so much so, that I have forgiven him face to face. I am now at the place where we can talk without me having hate and fear towards him but having genuine love towards him instead. It amazes me the power of forgiveness and the healing it brings to the victim and to the perpetrator. To be completely honest, I sometimes need to remind myself that I've even gone through that whole nightmare for it's not attached to me anymore.

Picture yourself going through a fire. Your hair and clothes would still smell like smoke hours later. But for me, it's like I have been through the fire yet there is not even a trace of the smell of smoke on me. That is how much cleaning up God has done for me. I like to think of it as being like a beautiful mansion that suddenly someone entered without permission and started to trash it by ripping the beautiful expensive carpets, smashing all the big windows and leaving the broken pieces all over the floor, going into the master bedroom and, with a knife, cutting all the pillows and bedding, destroying all the furniture, tearing down the walls…. making this PRICELESS mansion look worthless. And as a result, no one even wants to look at or consider this mansion, seeing how much work would be needed to fix it, and so the mansion is abandoned and left with no value. But then comes a Man who says, *"I am willing to put in the time and effort and the love to get this mansion up and running again. I remember how beautiful it was and how much potential it still has."* He buys the mansion with His Son. His Son has all the tools to fix this mansion and soon enough, with the right work, this once worthless mansion is restored back to its original beautiful state and is priceless again. But now, it is worth more than it ever was. That mansion was me, and it can be you, or any person who has gone through abuse. Someone has abused you without your permission and has ripped from you what was never to be stolen: your dignity, your purity, your value and much more. But just like the Man who saw potential in the mansion, God, in the same way, saw me and sees you. Even if you think you are a lost cause, He see the complete opposite; He see victory, freedom and redemption! You will make it! This is what I will be talking about in this book: Hope for a full victorious life.

CHAPTER 2

Hope for the Hopeless

"There is Hope." That is all I wanted to hear. I just wanted to know that I was going to be okay and that there was someone out there who had overcome sexual abuse. I knew in my heart that there was more for me, and I was going to do my best to be happy. All that I had been hearing though was the opposite. My therapists told me that no matter how old I would get or how happy I thought I was, that I would always be carrying my hurt around inside me and having flashbacks, but that I should accept it because it was NORMAL.

But if you have gone through any kind of abuse you know that flashbacks are NOT fun. They trigger panic attacks, depression, and much more. And this was what I had to look forward too? Wow! What a motivator for someone who had tried to end her life many times already! So, the 16-year-old-me felt hopeless and began to turn to other things to temporarily fill a void. I started to drink almost every weekend, whether at parties or just alone. I dated about eight guys within a one-year period. The more that I did things that I was not proud of, the more I felt empty, ashamed, lost, and hopeless.

Some of you may be wondering, "Wait! How did she tell someone she was sexually abused by her dad, and who did she tell? How did her family take it?"

There is so much fear that is put into girls and boys that are, or have been, sexually abused. And the fear is that no one will believe you if you speak about it. In my case, my fear was that my mom would abandon me and that I would be sent to foster care along with my brother. You fear for your life. I had kept it a secret for so long because I was scared that my mom would reject me and that my brother would be taken away from me. My father was such an abusive man, I honestly didn't know what all he would be capable of, and so I feared for my life.

But one day, everything changed forever. I had hit the bottom. I couldn't take it anymore. I grabbed a cable to end my life and as I started to choke myself, I whispered to God, "If you are there, take me to Heaven with You." When I said that, it was like a movie flashed right in front of my eyes. I could see my dad and mom finding me and my dad blaming my mom for my death. I saw my brother getting into drugs and ending up in jail. I let go of my grip right away, not wanting that to happen. I was laying on the floor so weak trying to get some air when my dad came in. He right away took me to the bathroom and started to splash water on me to wake me up.

His first words to me when I came to was, "What did your mom do to you again?"

Crying and pleading with him I said, "I might succeed one day! It's because of you that I have tried all these times to end my life! I need help! Please!" I begged him.

But he left me there and said, "No you don't. I have done nothing to you."

I realized that the little movie that I had seen was correct. He would have blamed my mom for everything. Hopeless, that night I prayed for the first time in a long time saying, "God, if You are out there, please let me know if I am wrong or if I am right. Let me know what to do because I am at my end." I went to bed that night and had a very realistic dream. I was running to the bus station near my house. In the dream, I had enough change to get on the bus, and I got out at the local Catholic Church where the priest was there waiting for me to tell him everything. He kept telling me that everything was going to be okay. The dream ended.

The next morning, my dad woke me up to tell me his "facts." "If you are under 18 years of age," he said, "and have gone through sexual abuse, you will be all over the news and be sent to a foster home different than the one your brother gets sent to. Your mom will be sent to jail and I will be too." He then asked me, "Is that what you want? Because if you come clean with this, this will be all your fault. Don't be selfish!" he said.

Then suddenly, I had strength that I'd never had before. It came up from deep within me. I said, "STOP IT! You know what? I AM going to be selfish! All these years, I have only been thinking of my mom and brother, but not anymore. I know they love me and I will fight to tell the police that my mom is innocent, and I don't care how long it takes! I am going to be happy, and I am not scared of you anymore!"

He replied, "You should be scared! No one will believe you!"

But I said, "No, I am not scared of you anymore. You should be scared of me and when I see you in court, you had better plead guilty! Look me in the eyes," I challenged him, "I am not scared of you, but I can see fear in YOUR eyes!"

I punched him hard in the face, so that he would let go of me, and I took off running. It was the middle of the winter - two days before Christmas. I ran so fast not knowing what to do. And then I remembered my dream. I needed to get on a bus. I began looking through my pockets to see if I had any change. I needed exactly $2.25 to get on the bus, but there was nothing in my pockets. I knew I needed to get on that bus. I was around the corner and shaking, not knowing what to do. I climbed onto the bus. Scared, I put my hands back in my pockets for the millionth time while the bus driver asked if I was okay. To my surprise I had exactly $2.25 in my right pocket! Still to this day, I have no idea how it got there but all I know is that it was God's doing. I sat down, and in keeping with my dream, I knew I needed to go to the church. I knew that there would be no turning back after this. I got to the church and I asked a lady where the priest from my dream was, and she said he was not there that day. She told me that there was another priest filling in for him. I told her that it had to be that specific priest, and I started to walk away, scared, not knowing what to do. How will I go back? Where would I go? Then I heard a voice as I was walking away. "Wait. Let me just take you into the office and see what we can do for you." As

I was waiting there, the lady suddenly turned back to me with a big smile on her face and said, "Here he is! I thought he had left for the day, but here he is!"

I was taken into his office. There I told him that I needed to give a confession. With a big smile he told me, "Okay, let's go into the church. I need to have a specific robe on for this." I walked with him and together we went to the confession room. I was shaking. He asked me, "Okay Alexia, what is your confession?" I told him that I was too scared to tell him and that if I told him, he couldn't tell anyone. He assured me that all confessions were kept in complete confidence. The priest saw how scared I was and so he told me that I could give my confession in Spanish if it helped, because God knew all languages and that he would be praying for me to have the strength to tell him later in English. I thought, Hey, now that is a deal! This priest knew no Spanish. Crying, I started to tell him everything in Spanish, but for some reason he was understanding everything I said! He told me, "Alexia this is not a confession. This is not your fault. There is no sin that you have done."

So that day I had already seen two miracles: money in my pocket that was not there moments before, and the priest understanding everything I said in a language he did not know! That same day, the priest helped me to tell my mom. She kicked my dad out of the house right away. She was so strong for my brother and I. After police interrogations and court hearings, my father ended up going to prison six months later.

After this devastating news, my mom soon turned to God and started to attend a Mexican Christian group that then led her to a Christian church. My brother and I, however, went drastically in the opposite direction - to the things of the world. We began to drink and date so much that it became a real issue. My mom then forced us to go to a Christian church that she had been attending. With a Latina mom you never say, "No", so hungover or not, my brother and I went. It had nice comfortable chairs and live music which we hadn't seen before.

After a few weeks of attending, a beautiful lady invited us over to her home for supper. My mom was so ecstatic because this lady had four Christian sons, and they all looked so happy, nice, and polite, and she wanted that for us. My mom, however, had to drag my brother to their house because he thought all Christians were boring. Besides, we were having to go on a Saturday evening - a potential party night! But when we arrived, we all felt such peace and a sense of safety. My guard was coming down already. They were serving chicken, rice, and vegetables for dinner, and like all polite hostesses, they let the visitors go first in line to get their food. So, I started to serve myself the tiniest portion of food on my plate because at the time, I was also dealing with eating disorders. The last thing I wanted to do was to throw it up at their house! How embarrassing would that be?! But one of her kids just grabbed my plate and said, "Oh come on! Don't be such a girl! Don't be shy!" and loaded my plate with food the size of a Viking's dinner! We all sat down and prayed before dinner. This was the first time I had ever seen that happen, especially done by a dad! I ended up eating all the food on my plate without even noticing because we were all having so much fun, talking and laughing.

After dinner, all four of their boys and my brother and I decided to go tobogganing while our parents stayed back. My brother and I had so much fun. We felt like children again! While out together, we began to ask them questions about why they didn't drink alcohol, and why they didn't have girlfriends, and many more questions. Their answers were so genuine and satisfying to us that it got us thinking.

Later that night when we returned home, my mom asked me, "What do you think of that lady and her family, but specifically that lady?"

I said, "Well, she is perfect. She has perfect kids, a nice husband, and seems so happy all the time."

Then she said to me, "Well what would you think if I told you that she has walked through a journey similar to yours?" I started to cry so hard because I could hardly believe it! There was the hope I needed! I knew it! I really could be happy!

I perked up and said to Mom, "Can we please call her? I want to talk to her now. Please Mom!"

So, the following day: Sunday, January 23rd, 2011 at about 8 PM, she came over to our house. She started to talk to me about things that I had never heard before, and she started to give me so much hope. She told me that she was so healed that she had to remind herself that she had ever lived in that, and that she had forgiven her abuser for all he had done. I was so amazed. How could this be possible? I so wanted what she had! "Alexia, you have tried everything else to be happy. Try God. He won't let you down. Trust me." she said with a huge smile on her face. And so, with my big fat ugly tears, I gave my life to Jesus right then and there! To my surprise, my brother also ended up giving his life to Jesus three hours later that same night! From that day on, I have never been the same. That day has changed my life forever - and for the better!

And watch this! I am also now married to this amazing beautiful lady's oldest son, and now have the most loving, caring, and funny father-in-law, who I consider to be much more than just the "in-law" part. He has been the first man that I have felt safe to hug, sit with, tickle, and be myself with. I know he loves me. Not once have I ever felt that he was looking at me the wrong way - the way my father had. He absolutely loves shopping, especially at stores that give you samples of food. We like to say that he has a reserved parking spot there for those with "Frequent Visitor Status". One time, he and I went together alone to do some shopping at this store, and it felt so good to go together! I felt so thrilled that, "Yes, this is my dad" ...that I almost called him Dad! He wouldn't have had any problem with it, but I held it back, and I thought, "Wow! God has filled a void in me that I didn't think even needed to be filled!"

You might be thinking, "Well Alexia, clearly you needed to fill this void because you had a horrible dad." But honestly, I never knew what a real dad was and because I never felt like I had one, I never thought that I needed one. I had gone all my life without a real father, even when he was around. But having the relationship I do with my husband's dad has honestly helped me to become more confident in myself and has helped me to grow in many areas of my life. Fathers have such an important role, one that they often don't even realize themselves. Mothers are not the only parents that kids need. They need their dads. Little girls need their daddies to feel safe, to feel beautiful, and to feel that they have value. They need their dads to help them to have healthy, strong standards.

So, there you have it! That is my long story about my past, written in short. So please, if you are in an abusive relationship, an abusive home, or any kind of an abusive situation right now, know that whatever is keeping you there is not worth it! There is so much more for you! You WILL be okay! You can trust the police. If you feel more comfortable going to your local church, they will give you all the help you need and more. Hear this loud and clear: NO ONE is allowed to or has the right to touch your body. You are priceless! NO ONE is allowed to manipulate you or make you feel worthless. You are not a piece of meat. You are not just another girl or guy. You are a beautiful creation from God, and you were bought at a price that is far greater than anything this world could ever offer you. You are loved, and you are NOT alone. The more that you keep the abuse inside of you, the heavier the burden will get and the more you will convince yourself that it is okay, and your fear will get stronger.

Yes, most times it is wise to take time to think through your decisions but this time just grab your phone, punch in the numbers, and dial. There is no going back to that life anymore, for you are one step closer to freedom! Sisters and Brothers, I am at this moment and each day of my life praying for you that God will give you the strength, that God will show you the way out, and that as He does, He will start to heal all your hurt! I have faith for you, and with you, for you to see God's unending love for YOU yourselves! To each of you, men and women of all ages, who have come out and told someone, I send you a big hug because I know it takes a lot of courage, and I know your pain. But now you are responsible for yourself! I am sorry to sound harsh but you need to crash down any pity parties! Go ahead and burn them down! Most often, after going through abuse of any kind, you can find yourself in a position where a lot of people begin to have compassion on you and will want to try to help you in any way they can. And yes, you will need a lot of support but make sure you don't fall into a self-pity pit, and as a result, become so dependent on people. Self-pity can be very ugly. It can lead to depression, bad decisions being made, and eventually to people distancing themselves from you.

What God actually wants for you is the opposite. He wants you to receive back everything that was stolen from you, multiplied by seven! And He's going to make satan pay for it, because after all, he's the one that was behind everything terrible thing that happened to you, not God! One of my favourite verses is ***"For the joy of the Lord is your strength." Nehemiah 8:10 NKJV*** Whenever I am feeling down, I have to remember that my best weapon to continue on each day is joy. For when I have joy, I also get the strength I need from God too! One thing I have also learned is the importance of reading the full context of what a verse in the Bible is saying. To do that, we need to go back and read the whole verse. So, let's do that.

"Then he said to them, "Go your way, eat the fat, drink the sweet, and send portions to those for whom nothing is prepared; for this day is holy to our Lord. Do not sorrow, for the joy of the Lord is your strength." So not only does God say that as we choose to have joy, we will also have strength, but He also tells us to enjoy our lives! Have fun! Take time to smell the flowers. Take time to laugh. Be with your loved ones, and STOP dwelling in the past! Don't live grieving! What will all that accomplish? Nothing. It will just be to your own destruction.

With that being said, I am not telling you that it is wrong for you to grieve at all because we do have feelings, and what you have gone through causes a lot of mixed emotions and a lot of hurt. But that will be healed if you will let God heal you.

In **2 Samuel 12:16**, we see that King David is "depressed". He had just been told that because of his sin, his son would die. And so, we see King David pleading to God for Him to spare his son's life. He refuses to eat, and he won't even get up from the ground. He is "grieving". But then in **2 Samuel 12:18**, we see that his little boy did die and then to everyone's shock, King David responds by getting up, washing himself, asking for food to be made, and then he goes out to worship the Lord. The people wondered, "What just happened? King David was in such a horrible state while his son was sick, and now that he is dead, he's okay?!" See King David's answer to this.

While the child was alive, I fasted and wept. I thought, "Who knows? The Lord may be gracious to me and let the child live. But now he is dead, why should I fast? Can I bring him back again? I will go to him, but he will not return to me." 2 Samuel 12:22 (NIV).

The reason I have even mentioned this passage of scripture is because we see here that there is a time for grieving but when that time has ended, it is unwise to stay there. Now let's take this passage of scripture and apply it to the suffering of abuse. While you were being abused and hurt, you were grieving inside and maybe even pleading with God and asking Him to help you - to save you. But now that you are safe, you may still be stuck in those emotions. They can almost make you feel safe because that has been your norm for so long. But you need to know that you ARE safe now. Yes, unfortunately the fact is that you DID go through those horrible experiences but that is done. So, flip the page and move on! I know it sounds "easier said than done" but if you don't start now, your healing process cannot begin. Keep pushing on. Eat. Get strong, and don't dwell in the past hurt. Take each day one at a time, and *"don't worry about tomorrow, for tomorrow will worry about itself." Matthew 6:32*

I know first-hand how self-pity can grab you and take you further and further into a pit that unfortunately, you are digging yourself. When I was in the midst of the abuse, I was in survival mode. So, I really didn't have time to grieve or to start my little pit. Then once it all came to the light, I started to dig...and digging like a professional. Not a lot of people knew my situation, but all my family did. My brother and my mom both got to the point where they were so tired of the "poor me act" that they stopped responding the way I wanted them to. My mom, with her stern Mexican voice told me, "Alexia, get out of bed! You are going to school whether you like it or not! I am done with your crying!" I was horrified. EXCUSE ME! I was at that moment hiding in my closet in a full-blown panic attack and I felt like my mom did not care! I did not feel that she loved me or that anyone loved me! But that day, I still didn't dare to say "No" to my mom. I STILL don't say "No" to my mom! You don't say "No" to a Mexican mom or the chancla will come out and it doesn't matter your age! (If you're Mexican, you will get it!) She gave me THE EYES, and I knew things had changed.

Today I know that what my mom did that day was actually the most loving thing she could have ever done for me. She pulled me out of my pity party and helped me to stop digging. It did not feel good at all at the time, and I did not see it as loving at all, but later I did. I am so glad that I had people in my life who pushed and pulled me even when I didn't want them to.

One day my brother came up to my bedroom and told me something I have never forgotten. "Alexia, I love you so much but you need to stop. You need to change your life or no one will be able to be around you. Look at it this way," he said "there are people in far worse situations than you." Then he started listing what sounded like extremely dramatic movie-like situations, but it opened my eyes to see that it was true. I was not the only one! I could do this! And now I am telling you the same thing. There is a huge cheering squad cheering you on. You can do this! You are not the only one who has gone through trauma, and you are not alone.

CHAPTER 3

Was It My Fault?

Guilt: The fact or state of having committed an offense, crime, violation, or wrong, especially against moral or penal law.

Are you feeling guilty? Can you even look at yourself in the mirror? Do you feel all alone and as though your pain is just so great that you just need to quit? Do you feel like you are screaming on the inside but nothing is coming out - that no one can hear your screaming? Do you feel as though you can't even cry anymore and that you are just going through the motions without feeling any emotion at all? Do you feel like you are numb and just drifting along? And then when you can finally feel emotions, do they rage like a storm with no mercy?

Well you are not alone. I can tell you that I went through every single one of those things. All those emotions - sometimes all of them at once - and then sometimes feeling so zoned out that I could not hear, think, feel, or even remember what I had done in the previous few days. I was there, but not really there. It is so hard to describe that feeling but it is one of the worst feelings there is.

I could not even look at myself in the mirror because I just felt ugly, and dirty, and all I saw was filth. When I would shower, I would try so hard to wash away the dirt and the filthy feeling I had. I would scrub and scrub, wash my hair a million and ten times, but it never seemed to go away no matter how hard I would scrub and no matter how many times I would shower! Even though no one actually knew, I felt that everywhere I went everyone saw me as "that girl" - a pity case - and that they could see all the filth that I was carrying. I would cry at night wondering who would ever love me, or who would ever care for me. I was broken, and I felt worthless. Most nights I was blessed if I was able to get more than 2 hours of sleep due to the nightmares and the tormenting fear of being hurt again. All these feelings were so real and suffocating! Then there were times when I would blame myself. Could I have done something differently? What if I dressed a different way? Was this something I deserved? Why me? It must have been my fault in some way or another for my dad to do what he did, and for it to have lasted as long as it did.

When I finally came out with the truth of what had been happening, the police told me over and over again that it was not my fault. They assured me that my dad was just a very sick man. Yes, that was very true, but I somehow still did not believe them. All those years of believing a lie makes it hard to just flip the switch. But let me share with you how I overcame those suffocating feelings - how I was able to flip the switch! Every night I would say **"When you lie down, you will not be afraid; Yes,** *you will lie down and your sleep will be sweet."* **Proverbs 3:24 (NKJV)** and I would whisper something that one of my favourite Authors and Speakers, Lisa Bevere, said: "Ask God to sing you a lullaby and put to sleep everything that has been awakened before its time." And I would finish with, "God, I trust You and I know You love me." Before I knew it, I was having the most restful sleep I had in years! To this day, I can happily say that I have not had one nightmare since. I now sleep like a bear and the joke now is that I have a gift for sleeping anytime, anyhow, and anywhere! Kaleb is the one that wakes up during the night when the girls do, I don't even notice.

Then every morning, I would go right to the mirror and read something that my now mother-in-law wrote out for me. I would feel so silly but I would tell myself,

> "God loves you Alexia. I am loved in Heaven and
> I am loved on the earth. I am beautiful, for I have
> been made in the image and likeness of God. I am
> fearfully and wonderfully made. God adores me. I
> am His treasure. I do not need a man to complete
> me. I am complete in Jesus. I am God's daughter
> and He delights in me. I am an heir of God and
> a joint-heir with Jesus. I am worth so MUCH! I
> can do anything. I have gifts, talents and abilities
> given to me by God and there is nothing I cannot
> do. Jesus loves me. And God loves me as much
> as He loves His own Son Jesus. Because of that
> truth, I am worth the very best. I love the Lord

my God with ALL my heart, with ALL my soul, with ALL my mind, and with ALL my strength. And I love others as I love myself, but I do not need other people to complete me. Jesus does that for me. I am complete and content in Him." *(I would recommend you copy this and make it personal to you or to write up something like this to take as your medicine every day).*

Little did I know that on those days when I was feeling so silly speaking all that to myself while not yet believing any part of it, I was actually speaking to my spirit. I was talking to my heart that had been broken and I was speaking life to it! One day after months of me constantly speaking this to myself every day, something awoke that had been dead in me, and a lioness came out! I looked at myself in the mirror and with a loud voice I shouted,

"I SILENCE any lie you have told me, you STUPID devil! Because I believe it now! Ha! I AM beautiful. I AM priceless. I AM loved. I AM a child of God! Everything that was meant to harm me is now turned around for my good, and no weapon, I tell you devil, NO weapon formed against me will prosper, because YOU are defeated, and you'd better be scared of me! I have a voice and I am not ashamed to use it anymore! I AM LOVED! I AM HAPPY! I AM NOT ALONE! And best of all, GOD IS BY MY SIDE!!!"

Now I tell myself in the mirror, "Hey GIRL, you got it going on! Today will be a great day! Shine God's light to all!"

Quickly after that, I began to realize my value and my worth and that feeling of dirt and filth started to fade away. I felt clean, I felt loved, and most importantly, I felt happy with who I was. I started to discover who I was, what I wanted to become, and I started to enjoy my life. Finding my value in God helped me to realize that my dad's decisions were not MY fault and that, yes, he was a sick man who needed help. I recognized that there was nothing I could have done differently to change my dad's decisions. When I came to this realization, I was able to finally forgive myself and that was another step closer to my complete and total FREEDOM.

Like a miracle cream that can take away all wrinkles if used night and day, I took the Word of God. Night and day, I was doing something that the Bible calls "renewing the mind." That means to change the way that you think to agree with what God said about you in His Word. It is taking any situation in front of you and seeing what the word of God has to say about it, and then to choose to agree with that and to keep saying THAT, until you begin to really believe it on the inside of you.

I am very visual so I always have these illustrations in my mind for everything I learn and the illustration of renewing of the mind came to me as a fairy tale. Imagine... a very young princess who gets away from her castle and gets lost. The king and queen send a search party for her but there is no sign of her. The princess is so young, lost not knowing where to go she begins to be raised in the streets, begging for food every day. Years go by but the king never loses hope. Every day he walks through the village in the hope that one day his little princess will come running into his arms. Then one day the King is out for his usual walk when he sees a girl full of dirt with torn clothing. He sees her begging for food with tears coming down her cheeks. He approaches her to give her some silver when he suddenly recognizes her resemblance to him. He is so excited because he knows he has just found his daughter! He brings her to the castle where everyone rejoices with him! They wash the dirt away, exchange the torn clothes for a beautiful gown, and they invite the whole village for a feast to celebrate her return! It all seems like a dream to her. But a day later, she puts her old clothing back on and goes back to earning her keep. She is out working in the fields when her father, the king, comes to her and says, "Sweetheart, you are a princess. You can wear anything you want. You can eat anything you want whenever you want, and you don't have to earn it or work for it. It's your inheritance! It's your birth-given right!"

While imagining this story, we can all understand that as a princess, she is not poor and does not need to beg for her food. She's had her inheritance from the very start. But for her, for so many years her identity as a princess had been stripped away and so it would take time for her to get used to her new life and to change her way of thinking. Changing your thinking, or "renewing your mind" takes some real time and intentional effort especially when there has been abuse and as a result, you have never felt safe, protected, loved, valued, or beautiful having had your identity stripped away. But it's time for you to begin your walk to freedom by changing the way you think! Grab hold of all the scriptures you need, find someone you can trust, and start this journey today! How do you do it? Google can be a great help! You can type out exactly what you want in the search bar, for example, "fear Bible verses" or "who does God say I am?" Then pick a few that apply to your situation. Write them down on cue cards or whatever works best for you, and begin to read them over and over. Soon, you may even have them memorized! I literally had Bible verses taped to my ceiling so that at night, I could just turn on my light and read the scriptures. The key is this: Let the Word of God do its work in you, because as you read it and make a choice to believe it even when you don't feel like you believe it, God's powerful Word will go to work and heal you and change you. But you must do your part and read them every day, expecting it to work.

Chapter 4

Confused Love

LOVE: *A profoundly tender, passionate affection
for another person, a sexual passion, or desire.*

I am going to talk to you about something most people either try to "sugar coat" or avoid talking about all together. "What is it?", you must be wondering. It's LOVE! But why is love something people want to avoid talking about? It is because they are simply embarrassed to talk about it openly and honestly. But I feel that it is something that is very important for me to talk to you about - to help "heal the word LOVE". The very definition of the word love is "a profoundly tender, passionate affection for another person." And the dictionary also goes on to describe it as "a sexual passion, or desire."

But why does Love always seem to be linked to sex somehow? Our world has done that. Our world has made love to be perverted into something that it is not. The world says that it is okay to have sex whenever you want, to whomever you want, at whatever age, and with absolutely no commitment required. An accepted mindset is that if you have not had sex or been in a romantic relationship, you are weird and you are now in the "one in a million bunch". I always say to young girls that it used to be the case that men had to pay women to have sex with them, but now women just freely give up their bodies with no value to themselves. But why is this? What changed this? It comes down to our self-worth and how we see ourselves. To correct that, you are going to have to do what I talked about in chapter 3 and what the Bible refers to as: Renew your minds. Change your thinking. Then once again, you will be able to see yourself the way God sees you, and the way many others still see you: WORTHY, PRICELESS, and BEAUTIFUL. In particular when you have gone through abuse, that can have been ripped away from you, but let's get back what was stolen from us!

When you have been abused, your concept of love and sex changes. Often one of the following occurs: a person chooses to become gay or bisexual, a person enters into a ridiculous number of relationships or they avoid the relationship commitment part entirely to just be "friends with benefits", a person ends up marrying the wrong guy/girl, and often some people find that they now want a lot of sex, or no sex at all. These are the things people don't want to talk about. I will be talking about each of these things in the order I have listed them and why they happen.

For some victims of abuse, they find themselves gravitating towards the sex opposite to the one they were abused by out of fear and a greater feeling of safety with the sex who did not abuse them. Or sometimes if a person is abused by the same sex, they then find themselves gravitating toward that same sex because the abuse wrongly created a sexual desire for that in them. This sometimes happens when abuse occurs at a younger age. It confuses a child's perspective.

As a woman, I can relate to women in this aspect but if you are a male reading this book, I hope you can find some common ground because I want to be as real as I can be. Because the abuse began at such a young age for me, my understanding of sex was extremely messed up. It corrupted my thinking. Little Alexia of age 7 started to have sexual activity with other little girls, because to be honest, I thought that was the way little girls played. I had seen it on TV. What I did not know was that the TV my dad was making me watch was called porn, and what I saw there was very wrong and NOT normal! That was how my father made me believe that what he wanted was normal, using the TV to confirm to me that everyone did those things. I thought every little girl played like that with their fathers and that it was a way that a daughter could show him that she loved him. He also showed me a grown man with a younger girl and told me that they were father and daughter. As I grew up, I figured out that this was not normal at all and that it was actually extremely WRONG! When I started high school, I considered myself bi-sexual because I would "experiment" with girls but still really like guys. I still really wanted a boyfriend. I wanted to be told that I was beautiful and I wanted to feel special. In high school, it was considered "hot" to have kissed a girl but to still like boys. So, because it was socially acceptable, I continued. I would not have sex with the girls, but I would play around with girls. I felt safer with them than with guys.

My mom had raised me with good morals and so even while my dad was still around, I discovered early on that without any kind of sexual affection, a man would not like you or stay interested in you. So, after that, I did not date at all until the truth about my abuse came out. That year, my actions became out of control. I began to drink a lot, an unhealthy amount, had a numerous amount of dating relationships and "friends". Eating disorders started for me then as well. It was honestly one of the worst years of my life as I faced what I thought was going to be my new reality. I now wanted to fill a void that had been there for so long, and so whenever a guy said I was beautiful or made me feel special, I was swept off my feet. I had a few "friends" before my first longer relationship of a whopping 4 months. At this point, I had not had sex with anyone apart from the abuse. I found out I was believing a lie that saying YES once meant you had to say YES all the time (sexually, or in many things really). Huge pressure may make you come to believe that, but it is such a lie. The truth is you are in control. If you said yes once to sex or even to a kiss, it does not mean you have to say yes again, nor does it mean you have to go further then you are comfortable with. It is as simple as this: if he or she does not respect your decision, you can just break that relationship off and walk away.

Because I did not know this truth, I found myself in this very situation, and immediately after, I would feel so ashamed, crushed, and disgusting. Due to the abuse I had gone through growing up, I had no memory of these encounters. At times like that, my mind would literally shut down. The police and the doctor later told me that was normal and that it was something my body automatically did to protect itself. Because it hadn't even been a year since my dad had abused me, my mind did that exact thing.

I honestly never thought I would get to experience love the right way, the way I thought I had seen it in the movies. I never thought I would be loved for who I was instead of what a man wanted me to be, or instead of an image the world had created. But once I turned my life over to God, the first thing He started to show me was how much He loved me. Then He showed me how much I was loved by my family and my friends, and then He began to show me how to love myself and to be happy with who I was. God gave me hope that one day I would have someone that would treat me and love me the way God would want His daughter to be treated and loved. I started to have standards and expectations. I made a decision to not date anyone until God showed me the one, He had for me. To remind myself, I wore a purity ring. I made a "LIST" and wrote down all the things I wanted in a man. It ended up being two pages long, double sided! Does not sound picky at all! But I knew I needed that to always go back to, and to believe God to give me the desires of my heart.

As I said at the beginning of the book, God did have a man for me that was MADE just for me from the beginning of time! He honestly fit every single thing I wrote on my list apart from one thing, and that one thing God revealed to me would always be a reminder to me of my father, and God didn't want one trace of my dad in my husband. God knew better, and I am so thankful for that! Kaleb and I have the best marriage! I know I am biased but he loves me in a way that I never thought would be possible. He loves me more than I have ever seen in another couple, more than I have ever seen in movies, and more than I could ever have imagined. I am so thankful to God for that!

Some of you who are married and have been sexually abused might be thinking the most obvious question: Has your sexual life been negatively affected? The answer to that is a big fat NO! I told God, "I have done everything You have asked me to do. I have forgiven my dad, talked to him on the phone and talked to him in person - all when You asked me to. And so, I am asking for one thing: that my marriage have no trace of my dad in it, and that my sexual life with my husband be pure and without any flashbacks. Oh, and I want my virginity back. Everything that was stolen from me, I want it back."

I don't know how, but I can tell you that I had proof the first night after our wedding that God had done what I had asked and I had been physically made a virgin again, and to this day there has not been even one second of flashbacks or any impurity of any kind in our lives. We both remained pure until our wedding night. Kaleb respects me and always has, and I can be "me" around him.

It is very important to stay pure in all things in your life, even in your marriage. That means you do not watch porn, together or separately. No role playing. Why? Because you need to be happy with each other, and not attempt to play out a fantasy or to look a certain way to please the other sexually. The world likes to tell you what your sexual life should look like but the world is wrong. God made sex. He made it to be pure and powerful as a man and woman join themselves together. Let your spouse be happy with all of YOU, not some fantasy they have in their minds. My husband does not watch porn and there are those who have said that it is not normal. Every guy watches it, they say. Well they shouldn't. As a wife, how would that make her feel, and how does it make her feel to know that her husband watches that? It makes a woman feel like she is not enough, when she is! I know this because you will remember that my dad made me watch pornography from a very young age. I got addicted to it, and every time I was done watching it, I felt dirty. I felt shame and guilt and that it had a strong hold on me. Nothing that is good should make you feel like that!

When I gave my life to Jesus, that is something that He just completely got rid of for me. Instead, it became disgusting and wrong. I began to feel compassion for the girls in the videos. Sometimes these things do not just vanish from one day to the next, but God can do anything! Perhaps with me it was. This girl has so many things that need to be done. Let's just take this one from off your pile. It may disappear right away, or you might need to work on this by renewing your mind with the Scriptures. You will need God to give you His strength to overcome this. Do not forget that when you have Jesus, you no longer need to rely on yourself. You are given the strength of God. When you choose to do your part, don't be upset if you get thoughts tempting you to go online to look up old websites. That is the enemy trying to get you to trip up, so just don't cooperate with him. As soon as the thought comes to your mind, tell him, "Be QUIET devil" and he will. (If you are interested in more about this subject, John Bevere has a great teaching on it called Porn Free.) Let God transform you!

A little shout out to all the single people out there reading this book! You may think that this does not apply to you. Well one day it will, and it is good to have your standards put in place. You are worth the very best. So, change your mind and do not put the responsibility of finding your spouse yourself. Trust God to bring your spouse to you! You are not supposed to be searching, you are supposed to be waiting and working on yourself in the meantime. Having faith in Him. I truly believe that God has one person for each of us from the beginning of time. When He created us, He also created our partner in life. So, He knows exactly where they are, what they are doing, and how He will bring them to you - if you will let Him. He did part the seas so I am sure He can make sure your paths cross! Be patient because God knows best! He knows the timing for you. He knows when both of you are ready to make a commitment and to be together forever. In the meantime, enjoy your singleness. Ask God to help you to take back what was stolen from you. Cooperate with God so that you can make sure you are living free. You do not want to bring wrong things into your marriage...

There is a very important subject that I need to touch on: Soul Ties. In particular for this book, I want to address the ungodly soul ties that can form between two people due to willing or unwilling sexual activity. Simply put, soul ties are emotional bonds that form an attachment. They may be godly or ungodly, pure or impure. A "soul tie" forms between two people who have participated in things that cause them to become attached or joined together in their souls. It is possible to have them form when a person gives their heart to another person as well. And that can be a good thing or a bad thing, depending on the situation. God has designed it such that right soul ties form within a marriage. But outside of marriage or in random dating relationships, they can be a real problem. Often you will hear people say, "I slept with him months ago but sometimes I still feel connected to him as though it was just yesterday." Soul ties. And the problem is, they do not just disappear over time. And real bondage can come with that.

Let me explain it like this: Imagine you have a piece of paper and you crazy glue it to another piece of paper. When it's dry, you try to separate the two pieces of paper. What happens? It's going to rip. And there will be sections of the first paper still attached to the second one and vice versa. Now imagine one paper is you and the other is someone you have been with sexually. God has designed it that two people become one flesh when they are joined sexually. Can you see the gravity of this? The other person takes parts of you, and you take part of the other person. You are no longer whole and you feel as though you are still attached to that person when you don't want to be. Soul ties. But don't be scared. It can be fixed with God! You can take back to yourself all that belongs to you, whether it was taken from you or given willingly. And you can give back to the other person all that belongs to them, and sever that soul tie forever. I personally had to cut all ungodly soul ties with my dad and with boyfriends that I had had. I also had to break ungodly soul ties with girls from my childhood where there was inappropriate behaviour and where ungodly, unhealthy, emotional soul ties were formed. How do you do this? It's so easy. I have included the prayer that I used below and at the back of the book and all you simply have to do is to pray it and mean it in your heart. Take a few minutes and think about who you might be needing to break soul ties with, and make this prayer personal to you. But remember, the power to do it only comes from God. So, this prayer will not have the same power to work in your spirit, soul (mind), and body without Jesus in your life. The power to do it is in the name of Jesus, and you cannot use His name if you don't belong to Him. But if you are ready to make this the day that you choose to let Jesus take over your life and invade you with His love, I have included a Prayer for Salvation that you can read out loud. Mean it with all of your heart. If you are not ready yet, that's okay! When you are ready, you can come back and pray the Salvation Prayer when you are. Then you will be ready, as well, to pray the second prayer below to break all ungodly soul ties. Please understand that all of the prayers that I have included in this book, except for the Prayer of Salvation, will only work for those who belong to Jesus. Not belonging to Jesus does not mean He does not love you or care for you, for He does. What I mean is that once you pray the prayer of salvation you now have given Him permission to work in your life and for there to be power in His word and in your prayers. You have become "HIS", his daughter or son. It is so GOOD to BELONG to Him.

Prayer of Salvation

Dear Jesus, I admit that I need You in my life. I have done lots of things wrong, and I ask You to forgive me for all of it. I choose to believe in You. I give my life to You now. I ask You to do something with it. Thank you for going to the Cross for me and for doing all that You did for me there. From this day on, my life is Yours. Thank you for loving me, forgiving me, saving, healing, and prospering me. I am Yours. Amen.

Breaking Soul Ties prayer

In the name of Jesus, I sever all <u>ungodly</u> spirit, soul, and body ties with _____ (name the person) I take back to myself any part of me that was connected to him/her. I give back to him/her any part of him/her that was connected to me.

I now sever with the Blood of Jesus all ungodly spirit, soul, and body ties with _____ (name the person again). (You can repeat this for however many times is needed)

Let God fight for you and with you to take back what rightfully belongs to you! Take back the control that was taken from you! Let Him turn the bad into Good. That is just who He is and what He does, if you will let Him! I am 5.3" tall and Mexican. There is absolutely no way that can be changed. (apart from high heels, of course.) Snow is cold, and fire is hot. You can't change that no matter how amazing it would be to be able to be in beach weather with snow all around you. In the same way, God cannot be changed. He is good. It's just who He is! He is a good God who wants to turn your mess into a masterpiece, your pain into joy, and your tears into laughter, for He gets no greater joy than to see us living a victorious life!

CHAPTER 5

Forgive the Unforgivable

"Don't even mention the word forgiveness again, he doesn't deserve it and I refuse to forgive him!" That is what I used to say. Most people would say, "I totally understand and wouldn't expect any less. You are right. Your dad doesn't even deserve your time let alone your forgiveness!" I liked to side with those people, and I thought they truly loved me and that they understood what I was going through. Who in their right mind would think that I would need to forgive my dad?! I didn't want him back in my life! I felt rage and hate rising in my blood, and my heart would pound in fear at just the thought of forgiving my dad. Just the thought of my dad at all produced that in me! I saw him as a horrible monster that I feared would find me and kill me after leaving jail. I was now able to express my feelings without having to hide them.

When my mom became a Christian, my brother and I were still living in hurt and confusion. The year that the abuse came to light (which was only 2 days before Christmas), I had the most horrible panic attack combined with an attack of such anger that my mom was so afraid for me that she drove me right over to the home of her new friends. I was barely able to breath and when I could, I was screaming at the top of my lungs, pulling out my hair, kicking and crying - all at the same time. We arrived. Her new friends were able to calm me down. They spoke very kind and calming words to me. They were my mom's Christian friends who were also Mexican. And they had Mexican food! To this point, my mom had never cooked in her life; my dad and the maids had been the cooks. So, when he left, so did our good food. He also left my mom with some big debts, so after paying rent and the bills, she was left with only 20 dollars in the bank which meant she would go without eating so that we could. So, if her friends gave us some food, none, raw, or burnt, we had to eat it no matter what it was! As I was calming down and starting to enjoy my time with them, they spoke the words I hated to hear: "Alexia, you have to forgive your dad to be free of these panic attacks."

You thought this would be the happy ending, didn't you? Well, you are wrong! Sweet little Alexia went a little crazy and told them off in a very horrible way, which I am still not proud of! I asked them, "How can you tell me to forgive my dad when you have no idea what I have been through and how horrible a man he was to me?! You have NO idea!" From what I could see, they were taking my dad's side so I made my mom drive me home where I locked myself in my room. I cried with so much pain in my heart just thinking of everything that I had lost: not having my dad ever walk me down the aisle at my wedding or being there when I graduated or being there when I had kids. I felt that I was the reason why my mom would be alone with her dreams of growing old with her husband, thrown out the window. I felt that I was the reason my brother would never have a dad to teach him how to fish, switch a tire, and do all the father/son things. As I was on the floor crying, I prayed to God for the second time, "God, I am done. Everyone tells me I won't ever be fully happy - that I will be like someone who has lost a leg or an arm and that though I would learn how to function without that limb, it would always be a constant reminder. I don't want that for my life! I want to succeed! I want to be happy! If you are real and care about me, send me someone who can give me hope!"

And just like that, the next week I met the beautiful lady that ended up being my mother-in-love. As she was sharing her story with me, she told me that one of the most important steps in becoming happy and free is to forgive. This time it was different. This time that advice was coming from a lady who had lived in what I had, and she had what I wanted. Finally, I was ready. That night, I chose to forgive my dad and I knew I couldn't do it alone, so I asked God to come into my heart and for Him to give me His strength to do it. I felt like a huge weight was lifted from my shoulders! My heart felt happy. My mother-in-love explained many things to me that night and told me that I could talk to Jesus about anything I wanted, even things I needed to just rant about to let them out and let them go for part of my healing. *(For even to this day the only people that know all the details of my abuse are the detectives, my dad, me and now God, for I knew if I told anyone I would just hurt them with the details. So, I kept it all, until I talked to God, I put a chair in front of me and visualized Him listening to me.)* That night after she left, it was around 3 AM when I went to bed, and with NO FEAR! I knelt by the side of my bed because that's how I had seen it done in movies. The truth is there is no wrong or right position to pray. In fact, my preferred way to pray now is to walk around with my eyes wide open. And it seems the best time I hear God is actually in the shower! Instead of just singing in the shower, I also pray to God in the shower! But back to that night: As I knelt, I asked God that if He was real, could He could show me and then I would never doubt Him again. I knew I could ask this because His word said this:

Psalm 25:14 NKJV
"The Lord confides in those who fear Him; He makes His covenant known to them."

Matthew 7: 7-8 NKJV
"Ask, and it will be given to you; seek, and you will find; knock, and it will be opened to you. For everyone who asks receives, and he who seeks finds, and to him who knocks it will be opened.

For the very first time I felt inside of me a message that was so strong and so real saying. "I love you Alexia and I was there while you wept. I wiped your tears. I never wanted this to happen to you. I love you, my daughter. Trust Me! He will never hurt you again." Just that simple and powerful message was everything I needed to know and ever needed to know!

If God is for us, who can be against us? 32 He who did not spare His own Son, but delivered Him up for us all, how

shall He not with Him also freely give us all things? Romans
8: 31-32 NKJV

That is right! GOD IS FOR ME AND NOT AGAINST ME!
I can trust His perfect plan for me. That day was the beginning of
a new life for me. After that, everything was amazing and I didn't
have to deal with any anger or pain ever again... MY HAPPILY
EVER AFTER...NOT! That is honestly how people make it
seem but there is pain... a lot of pain. There is a lot of working
through things. The difference is that now you are not alone; you
now have strength that you didn't have before and it has been
given to you for free. Why do I keep repeating that over and over
throughout this book? Because I need you to keep hearing it so
that you can see how it is so simple, yet so important.

The next day, I still felt the same whenever I thought of my
dad or his name was mentioned. My heart would race and I would
feel the panic attacks starting. But I would remind myself that I
had forgiven him and that I was not alone. Then I honestly felt
better and had so much peace. BUT then not even ten minutes
later, I would get a trigger or flashback and the hate started to
pump through me, and again I would remind myself that I had
forgiven him and that God was with me now. I had to do this 100
times a day sometimes! Slowly it became 50 times, then 25, then
10 and now it is once in a blue moon. It's okay if your feelings
feel so real and you don't "feel" like you have forgiven because
that's not your job. Your job is just to choose to forgive and then
to keep reminding yourself that you have already forgiven that
person, and I can promise you, God will take it from there! And

He will take care of your emotions and your heart! He does what only He can do. He restores and mends everything that was broken and somehow makes it better than it ever was before! I can't tell you the science behind it or the secret. All I can say is that it works! God gets inside of you and starts to wipe away the hurt and clean away all the bad memories that are in your mind. He starts to replace it with His love, peace, comfort, and much more. It is something only He can do. Imagine a sponge that had been used to paint something and is now soaked in black paint. You need to clean it out and so you put it under the tap and you soak it and squeeze it out, soak it and squeeze it out. You repeat the process adding soap until the water coming out is no longer black but clear. Now imagine you are that sponge. The black paint is the hurt. The water is God, and the soap is the Word. The more you keep soaking yourself in God and His Word, the cleaner and freer you become. Now people can see it on you and in you! I am literally crying right now as I am typing this! It is such a freeing feeling knowing that you are being cleansed and that the excruciating pain is being removed. You are being wiped clean and given a fresh new start. And now you can choose whatever paint colour you want!

But don't forget, God is real but so is the devil. So, as you are allowing God to supernaturally change you from the inside out, the devil will try to make you think you are still a sponge covered in black paint, and old emotions may try to creep back in - the flashbacks. The devil has stolen enough from you, so don't let him lie to you that you are not really CLEAN. He has NO right to take the beauty that is inside of you. Don't let the devil tell you lies. You just say, "Be QUIET devil! You are the father of all lies and so now I know that whatever you are trying to tell me, the opposite is actually true! You say I am alone, afraid, ugly, unworthy, will never overcome, will get hurt again, won't ever be free, and that God doesn't care. But now I know the opposite is true! I am PRICELESS, BEAUTIFUL, WORTHY, LOVED, FREE, an OVERCOMER, a VICTOR, and I am NOT ALONE, and GOD DOES LOVE ME! Let the devil be scared of you from the moment you wake up and even while you sleep!

As I continued to walk this journey for about three months, God showed me in a dream that I was going to be talking to my dad on the phone and that I was going to be telling him that I had forgiven him. I thought, "HA! That won't happen! He's in jail!" So I agreed and said, "Sure." But then there is God being God, which I have come to notice that He can make ANYTHING happen! Later that week, I went to my grandmother's house (my dad's mom) to visit my 100-year-old great-grandfather and to have lunch with him...when my dad called the house! Right then and there, I remembered the dream I had. It all came back to me. I was even wearing the exact same outfit as in the dream! As I sat on the chair, I felt as though I was a magnet stuck to it. My heart started to pound and I started to sweat. Then I felt that little tugging inside me saying, "Are you going to do it? Look at how much God has done for you. This is clearly what He is asking you to do." So, like in good Alexia fashion when I feel nervous about doing a thing, I quickly begin to do something so that there's no turning back. I quickly said, "Grandma I need to…" as I stood up out of my chair. Now it was too late to sit back down and pretend it never happened! I went on to finish my sentence by saying, "I just need to talk to my dad." Her eyes and face said it all! Both her and my father on the other end of the phone were as shocked as I was! Speechless, she handed me the phone. I talked to my dad, sharing with him the good news that I had given my life to Jesus and that I had forgiven him and hoped that he too could find God. I was very new at this so I also told him one or two things in a "not so loving way" about how the Bible says he will go to Hell if he didn't accept Jesus in his heart. In my mind, I was hoping maybe he would finally say that he was sorry, repent, give his life to Jesus, and then everything would be amazing - a happily ever after. He did say that he was happy to hear I was doing well, but then let me know about his treatment in jail and said that it was my fault that he was in there. I quickly corrected him, reminding him that his actions and his decisions put him there. Then just like a band-aid getting pulled off, the phone call was done. I did not understand why it didn't work out like I had hoped. The phone call had ended instead with me putting him in his place. But soon after having that thought, I GOT IT. I understood! I had regained the CONTROL that he had taken from me! I was now in CONTROL! For the very first time, his voice did not scare me or intimidate me. I felt like I was the queen of the hill! I felt as light as a feather, and I felt like I had conquered this huge giant! I now knew why God had asked me to do this! As the years have gone by, the feeling in my heart of having forgiven him became easier. I was a whole new person! I was finally happy and loving my life! I had forgotten my past and was enjoying my new one. I had new friends, a new job, and a new EVERYTHING. I had fully committed my life to God, and my life couldn't get better!

BUT…. then it came time for my dad to get released from

jail. Four years had gone by so fast, and the panic attacks and fear came rushing back, and rushing back so strong that I questioned everything God had done for me in those previous few years. What will my dad do? Will he be released from prison and come find me to kill me or abuse me again? I felt my confidence, strength, and control slipping through my fingers. My anxiety got so bad that I even had my co-workers walking me to my car. I didn't want to be alone. I had my phone ready to dial 911 and, in my head, I had mapped out all the possible exit options. This was not living. I was living in absolute fear again. I was allowing him to control my life yet again.

The day came for his release. Once again God showed me in dreams, and visions, and showed me through His Word, the Bible, that I was to meet with him in person. My mind raced, "WHAT?! NO way! There was absolutely no way I would meet with him in person! Wasn't the phone call enough? First of all, he doesn't deserve it. He had never even apologized to me for what he had done, and I have to be the one to forgive him in person?" For 2 weeks I didn't even want to talk to God. I was in complete disobedience to His voice and I didn't want to listen to Him. But there is no running away from Him.

On Father's Day, my lead pastor was in the middle of his sermon when all of a sudden, he stopped and said, "I feel a very big urge in my spirit to say the following. I am not sure who it's for but I will listen to the Lord. There is a girl here that God has been talking to and she is not listening to Him. You have forgiven your father, but you need to tell him that you did." I literally ran out of the service to the bathroom, unable to catch my breath. "Bawling" is an understatement. I screamed to God, "I GOT IT DADDY!" He had been loud and clear enough and I didn't want to find out what would be next! So, I told God that I would listen to Him and obey. As always in my dreams, God had been so detailed and to the point that I even knew what I would be wearing. So, I knew where we were to meet and who all was to be there. In my dream, my other pastor was there and I told God that I wasn't going to ask him to come so He would have to work something out. He did. Right after I came back from my crying episode, my associate pastor (who is now lead pastor), Pastor Chad, told me that he wanted to talk to me. He said, "Alexia, I just want to tell you that if you ever want to meet with your dad, know that I will be there for you if you want me to be. Even if I am a pastor, know that you will be safe." The tears, as fast as they were gone, came back and I knew I had just had my last confirmation. I told him everything that had been going on leading up to that moment, and I called my dad not even 2 hours later. When I called him, I wished him a Happy Father's Day even if he did not deserve it. But I have come to learn that God wants me to act like Him, for His love can conquer everything and every situation. I actually said that! He agreed to meet with me at my church the following week.

As the day was approaching, I couldn't eat and I couldn't sleep. All I could think about was what he could do to me, how he would look at me, how he could manipulate my words. The night before I could not stop vomiting. I felt extremely weak and scared. I began to second guess myself. "This can't be what God is asking me to do? Surely!" But that next day, we went to the church, and we waited for him at my pastor's office. Pastor Chad said something that was so powerful and it changed the way I felt and saw the meeting. "Alexia, you now have all the control. You say when we start, and you say when we finish. It is up to you. When you want your father to be quiet, and when you want him to speak - it is up to you. This is your meeting and I am here to help and also to protect you." At that moment, I felt so safe and in control. I could do this. I asked him to send my father in. As he walked into the office, I honestly started to laugh out loud! I could not control it. "Alexia, control yourself!", I told myself! After I literally bit my tongue, I was able to stop my laughter. But why was I laughing? Because the moment I saw the man that I used to fear, this big monster that had haunted my days and nights, the one that had become bigger, scarier, and stronger in my mind, I saw for the first time that he was actually just a weak, fragile man. He was a man who could not hurt me anymore. At that moment I realized that God had me covered. There wasn't anything to fear any longer! My father had lost so much weight while in jail. For the first time I felt so much stronger than him and I felt in control. I now understood what God was up to.

When we sat down to talk to my dad, I had no idea that God's purpose for the meeting was to let him know that we had forgiven him individually and as a family. When my dad saw us, he realized everything he had missed - how much we'd grown up and how many significant life moments he had missed. The meeting was short but to the point. I also made sure my dad knew that in telling him that I had forgiven him, it did not mean that he was welcome back into our lives. There would be very specific solid boundaries in place regarding communication of any kind that I would be in control of determining. Even then, my heart's desire was that he repent and give his life to God. I understood that Jesus died even for the worst of the worst, and that though He hates the things they have done, He still loves them as much as He loves me. He wants them to repent so that they can be forgiven and live as free as He made me! I knew that the Bible said that it is not God's will for ***anyone to perish, but everyone to come to repentance. 2 Peter 3:9 NKJV*** *And I knew that God* ***desires all men to be saved and to come to the knowledge of the truth. 1 Timothy 2:4 NKJV***

After that meeting, I was no longer afraid to walk alone. Fear thoughts of my dad trying to kill me and the ways in which he would do it, no longer filled me. Sleep returned and once again, I could be completely free.

Sometime later, God put in my heart to meet with my dad one final time - when my husband and I got engaged. God kept speaking to me and reminding me that one of the commandments was to: ***"Honor your father and your mother, that your days may be long upon the land which the Lord your God is giving you." Exodus 20:12 NKJV***

Notice that this scripture does not say... ***Honour your father and mother so that you may have a long life, BUT only if they are good and have never done anything to hurt you.*** No, it just says to honour them so I knew I was going to have to do what God had asked for three reasons. First of all, I knew by now that God was going to have His way no matter what! Secondly, I wanted that long life, and then lastly, I knew how much freedom came from my obedience to obey God in it the past two times I had met with him. I did not want to miss what God had for me this time. My husband is a man of God, and he said that he also wanted to obey God and would come with me. So yet again for one last time, we packed up and travelled to meet him, but this time we would meet at a park - a more social spot. When we met with him, he approached us and said that he was so happy to see us. He then looked at the 6 foot 4 Dutch, well dressed, red neck next to me and said, "Hi. Who are you?" I told my dad that this guy was the reason I was there and that we were there to meet with him for the purpose of letting him know that we were getting married. I told him that we wanted to honour him as my biological dad. He clearly understood he was not invited to the wedding, but I could see in his eyes how he was starting to understand just how much his wrong decisions were costing him. We ended up spending a whole hour in conversation, laughing and enjoying our time.

Then my father said, "Alexia, I have had lots of time to try and think of any and all questions that you might have for me. So, ask me and I will answer anything you want to know." This is what I had longed for all my life. Finally, the words coming from his mouth, explaining himself. But here was the thing, God had already done so much in me that hearing his answers would do nothing for me anymore. What would his explanations accomplish? Nothing. What was done was done and there wasn't anything that could change that. Nothing he said would make me respond, "Oh, that totally makes sense!" There was absolutely no explanation or excuse for what he did. All I knew is that God had changed my thinking and helped me to see that he was a hurting man who couldn't help himself. He was in terrible bondage. To me, he was not my father anymore. God was. So, I released my dad and told him, "Dad, I have no questions for you. I don't need any of the answers you have come up with. I fully forgive you with no strings attached. I want to let you know that through the whole mess you created, I know you still loved me, and I love you too. You are my dad. I have always loved you. I pray you can forgive yourself." At that moment he was in tears, and with a very soft voice he said, "Thank you." That was it. We left. Later that day, he sent us a message to let me know how overwhelmed he was seeing how I had overcome and was able to share true forgiveness. He said that he knew it could not have come any other way than through God.

It's like I say all the time now from the bottom of my heart: ***"I am here to LOVE you and not JUDGE you!"*** It's so true! Love overcomes anything and can make a hard heart soft. Again, I had wished that then would have been the time that he repented and changed his life, but unfortunately, from what I know, he has not changed a bit. He is still deceiving people and even became engaged to a woman who had two little children. Don't worry! I warned her politely about my dad. He got very upset with me about it, and for a moment, I wondered what he might do to me. He said that I had ruined his life, and that I must not have fully forgiven him because a person who had, would have just encouraged his engagement. He had not told her about us or what he had done. For a moment, I started to question if I had truly forgiven him but I quickly snapped out that! I had done it politely and had just warned her for her children's sake, in particular, for her little girl who looked so much like me. I did not want to have that on my shoulders knowing that I could have done something. I also knew it didn't matter what he thought about my forgiveness. What mattered was that, in my heart, both God and I knew that I had forgiven him. After all, it is God who knows our hearts.

Understand something though. Just because I have forgiven him, does not mean that if he were to show up at my door that I would welcome him into my home. No! I would call 911. You still need to use wisdom. Please always use wisdom. Even when I did meet with him, I was never alone. There were always three other people there with me. And please understand something else. God specifically told me to see him in person, but that does not mean that He will ask you to do the same. But if He does, you can trust that you will be safe. Just make sure that you do not go alone. To this day, my dad has not come to accept Jesus. YET. But that's okay. I know one day he will because I pray for him every day, and I know that I have planted a good seed in his heart and that he has been able to see Jesus through our family.

I wanted to share with you my journey of forgiveness because I know it's not easy. But it is your ticket to freedom! Why not do it now? Remember that even if you do not feel like it, the feelings will come later! It's a choice! It is like choosing to go to work out at the gym. You will not likely lose all the weight you want that first day causing you to leave the gym looking like a supermodel! That would be amazing, but it's not how it works! You need to put sweat and work into achieving your goals. It is the same thing with forgiveness! Having your feelings agree with your choice to forgive takes time. And on top of it, it's so simple to do. All you have to do is to choose to forgive, to say it, and then to choose to trust that God will work out His promise. And keep the Word of God flowing into you!

I encourage you to repeat this confession of VICTORY. Let today be your day for FREEDOM!

I (your name) choose to forgive (person's name) for (say what the person(s) did) today. I choose to live in freedom and let go of this hurt. God, I pray for your strength and for your grace. Thank you Lord for I can trust in Your promises. It is finished, paid for, and given to me freely by the blood of Jesus Christ. Amen.

It is that simple and that easy. There is no formula. And just remember, when the feelings of hurt try to come rushing back in, remind yourself, "No, I have already chosen to forgive that person!" I am so excited to see all of you living in complete VICTORY! If I can do it, so can you!

CHAPTER 6

Why God?

God why? Why me? Why did You allow this to happen? Why didn't You do anything? Why don't You care? Why did I go through this? There are so many WHY'S! Have you ever asked why? God answered all of my "why" questions to help me to heal and to move on. I am going to tell you what He showed me, but I want to start by asking you a question. Do you think God created you to get abused? To be hurt? Just think about that. It's okay if your answer is "Yes" or "I think so" because that is what this chapter is about.

I asked God all the why's. Most of the hurt that I carried before and after I became a Christian had at its root the thinking: If You really care, or if You are so powerful, then how could You let this happen? God, you are supposed to know everything so why didn't You do anything? Why did You even create me? Like Alexia will go through a bunch of abuse for 14 years, have a horrible life, but around 17 years of age, her life will change and she will be okay. Or why did Hitler exist? Why allow him to be alive when you knew what he was going to do? You know everything, so why create him because look at all the damage he did?

I was almost afraid to hear the answer because I wasn't sure what God was going to say. But He answered me with His Word.

Isaiah 44:24 NKJV "Thus says the LORD—your Redeemer, And who formed you in the womb: "I am the LORD who makes all things, who stretches out the heavens all alone, who spread abroad the earth by myself."

Jeremiah 1:5 NIV "Before I formed you in the womb I knew you; before you were born I set you apart;"

Genesis 1:27 NKJV "So God created man in His own image, in the image of God He created him; male and female He created them."

Psalm 139: 13-14 NIV "For you created my inmost being; you knit me together in my mother's womb. I praise you because I am fearfully and wonderfully made; your works are wonderful, I know that full well. My frame was not hidden from you when I was made in the secret place. When I was woven together in the depths of the earth, your eyes saw my unformed body. All the days ordained for me were written in your book before one of them came to be."

God formed us in the womb in His own image...PERFECT! The story He wrote for us WAS and IS perfect without any climax or dramatic point like in a movie. It is a book that is full of "happily ever after" pages. The problem is that when we are born, we enter into a fallen world, a world of sin where people have free choice.

"Therefore, just as sin entered the world through one man, and death through sin, and in this way death came to all men, because all sinned—for before the law was given, sin was in the world...Even over those who did not sin." Romans 5:12-14 NIV

People have been given the freedom to choose life or death, blessing or cursing. Later in that same chapter, God goes on to say: *"But where sin increased, grace increased all the more, so that, just as sin reigned in death, so also grace might reign through righteousness to bring eternal life through Jesus Christ our LORD. Romans 5: 20-21 NIV*

"I have set before you life and death, blessing and cursing; therefore choose life, so that both you and your descendants may live." Deuteronomy 30:19 NKJV

God has left it up to us to make decisions every day to either do good or bad. He is pure love and will not force anyone to choose what He wants. He allows us to choose Him if we want, and all the good things that come along with choosing Him. Everyone has been given the freedom of choice. The problem is, if a person chooses to do bad (sin), unfortunately others get affected. In a mass shooting, no one accuses the crowd and says, "Well, why were you there anyway?" We know that the victims did nothing wrong! They were just busy with their normal daily activities: shopping, working, or going to school. But all it took was one sick person to affect thousands. To go in and shoot people was that madman's decision. And his horrible choice ended people's lives and hurt their families, friends, and the rest of the world watching. Your choice to SIN doesn't just affect you; it affects those around you too. ***Sin keeps you longer than you wanted to stay. It costs more than you wanted to pay, and it takes you farther than you wanted to go!*** So just like we make decisions as kids to not eat a cookie our mothers told us not to in order to avoid the consequences, as we become older, we make decisions to not do drugs, or drink and drive, or murder a person. Why? Because consequences come with our actions. A person might be able to get away with it for a while, but eventually the truth comes out.

"Therefore do not fear them. For there is nothing covered that will not be revealed, and hidden that will not be known." Matthew 10:26 NKJV

Every day we make decisions to do what is right and good, and every day we make decisions to do what is not good and right. We all have. For example, not too long ago, I chose to listen to my flesh. There was a person who had hurt and disappointed me. This person loves Jesus and is a sweet person but unfortunately, also being human, was not being so nice to me or to others. I didn't say anything for a long time and instead I chose to just to avoid this person. I have a hard time being fake and pretending there is not "an elephant in the room", but avoiding is not always the right decision. This person noticed that I was avoiding them and aggressively confronted me in front of A LOT of people. I tried to walk away from the situation knowing it was neither the time or the place. They insisted. So in private with them, I snapped. And though I had spoken the truth, I could see I had also hurt this person's feelings. I could feel my blood pumping and I knew I had messed up. Yes, this person had started it. Yes, this person would not let me walk away, but I still chose not to walk in love. I chose to react. I should have said, "When you have calmed down, we can talk." I could have just kept walking or even run if I had to! I could have, I could have, I could have. I instantly regretted how I had reacted but I also knew that I, too, am human. I make mistakes. Right away, I asked God to forgive me. I forgave myself, and I asked that person to forgive me for the way I had acted. Understand that sometimes you may ask a person to forgive you and they don't make it easy on you, but that is not for me to carry. I had asked this person to forgive me and now it would be their choice to accept it or not. I am a peacemaker and I HATE having people mad or upset with me, but I could not keep beating myself up over a choice I had made that God had already forgiven me for - an action He didn't even remember. I had peace knowing that I had done my part. In this I have also forgiven and let go and do my best to walk in love and see the best in this person.

It's times like these when the devil comes in and tries to steal your peace and joy. He tries to make you feel guilty and ashamed.

But I didn't let him. It was not easy. Every time I would feel yucky, I would have to remind myself that if God already forgave me and had chosen to no longer remember the incident, then why would I continue dealing with something that was not even on God's radar anymore? God was not responsible for the wrong way that I had gone about that situation. I had control over it to do what was right, or to not do what was right. I chose. But God still helped me after I repented. Why am I going into so much detail about something that seems so small? I wanted you to see how decision-making works so that you can see that God did not want and did not choose for the abuse, the hurt, or the pain to happen to you! That is not who He is! He has only ever wanted the best for you.

"For I know the plans I have for you," declares the LORD, "plans to prosper you and not to harm you, plans to give you hope and a future." Jeremiah 29:11 NIV

God's plan is to bless us and to prosper us, to give us hope and a future. So when someone else's wrong decision hurt you, He has been working His best to get you back to His good plan for you. He has you reading this book!

For me, God intervened by moving me back to Canada and then four years later, having me meet my husband's family and finding out about God's love! Now that I look back on my life, I can see that God was with me the whole time, even when I didn't think He was. I had dismissed two happenings in my life as nothing and just plain forgot about them. But God reminded me. The first took place while my dad was abusing me. I can remember it as though it was yesterday. I can visualise the whole scene in my mind. There he was doing what he was not supposed to, when little Alexia said, "Dad is it true that we all have guardian angels protecting us?"

He quickly responded, "Yes."

I went on to tell him, "Well I have two, and they are right beside me and they are very angry with you. You better stop."

His face was in shock and in fear. He pushed me off the bed and told me to leave the room right away. I had absolutely no idea what had just happened. I could see these big strong angels, and not like the movies like to say they are. They didn't have wings while wearing white bed sheets! NO! They were big and strong. I had totally forgotten about this until God reminded me on the night that I gave my life to Him. He was there. That night came rushing back to my mind. He had always been there all along.

The other most impacting and powerful "God-moment" for me was when I was seven years old. I was crying in my bed just wanting to end my life. I felt so hopeless and alone. All of a sudden, I could see light in my room but I knew that I hadn't turned the light on. So, I opened my eyes, and there beside my bed was a little girl with a beautiful, shiny, colourful dress. She was around my age and had such a big smile.

"Come with me." she said.

"Where?" I asked her.

Pointing to my window she said, "Up there."

"I can't go up there!" I responded.

She held her hand out to me and said, "Trust me."

I felt safe and I stretched my hand out to her. I noticed that she was floating and that we quickly left my room and we were suddenly in Heaven. I was playing, dancing, and eating everything I liked. I was having so much fun with a bunch of kids that I couldn't stop laughing and smiling. It was the best! It felt like I would be there forever! Not once did I think of anyone back on earth. In fact, I didn't think of earth at all! This was all I could think of and see: FUN! The little girl came back and took me to a massive table. Honestly, it was like thousands of people were gathered around this table just eating and loving life. Although there were so many people, it still didn't feel like the table was that big; it felt like a regular family dinner. I sat at the end of the table and as I was eating, the little girl came back and said to me, "He wants to see you." Hopping over, I was put on Jesus' lap. I couldn't see His face but He just radiated light, love, and safety. I knew it was Him, and I knew I was loved, and I loved Him so much! I knew I did.

I was told "Alexia, it is time for you to go back." Right then I remembered about earth, my family, and my dad.

"No, NO please don't send me back! PLEASE! I do not want to go back. I love it here!" I pleaded.

Before I knew it, I was back on my bed just like that. I knew in my spirit that I had to come back because I had things I needed to accomplish for Him." Then some I was back on my bed just like that. For many years I thought of it as a dream, a very nice dream, a dream that every time I thought of it, gave me comfort when I wasn't having a good day. Then somehow, I forgot about it. But God had not forgotten. And it was another thing that He brought rushing back to my mind the day that I gave my life to Jesus. I was then able to understand that it was Jesus, and that I had been given an encounter with Him. He had chosen me for this. Remember how I said I was given the message that there were things I need to do? This book is one of those things! He wants you to know who He is - a good, good Father. He is such a good Father who loves us so much that brought me back to share with you how to overcome; how to live FREE!

Another thing that really helped me to silence the "why's" was digging into and reading the Bible to find out who God was, who He is, and who He will always be. As I did that, I discovered that from day one, He has only ever wanted the best for us. I discovered that He loves us no matter our mistakes, and that He sent His Son - His ONLY son - for you and me. He sent Him to die for your sin and my sin and for everyone's sin. I want to dig deep into this because I want to convince you of God's love! I have fallen so in love with God that I can't be shaken with any other option or idea.

Everyone knows Abraham as being the father of all faith, Moses as being the deliverer of the Jews, Daniel as being the man that was not eaten by lions, Esther as the queen who delivered the Jews, and David as being the man after God's own heart. I could go on and on, letting you know about all the men and women in the Bible who are known for their greatness and the amazing works they did for God. But every single one of them that I mentioned to you, made wrong choices along the way too. They chose sin too sometimes. But why are they not remembered for their sin and how they failed? Because God chooses not to remember our past or our mistakes when we ask for His forgiveness. ***"Purge***

me with hyssop, and I shall be clean; Wash me, and I shall be whiter than snow. Make me hear joy and gladness, That the bones You have broken may rejoice. Hide Your face from my sins, And blot out all my iniquities. Create in me a clean heart, O God, And renew a steadfast spirit within me."
Psalm 51: 7-10 NKJV

One very key thing about being able to receive forgiveness from God is whether or not we have forgiven others. How do we expect God to forgive us when we have not done the same for others? We are to treat others the way we want to be treated. God asks us to forgive others so that we can be forgiven as well. WOW! Clearly, He knows the power of forgiveness! It is all for our benefit really. It is the ticket to freedom from guilt and shame and hurt. If we know we are forgiven for what we have done wrong, it takes a weight off our shoulders, and when we forgive others, we become free ourselves. I think God knows what He is doing!

"Therefore, as God's chosen people, holy and dearly loved, clothe yourselves with compassion, kindness, humility, gentleness and patience. Bear with each other and forgive whatever grievances you may have against one another. Forgive as the Lord forgave you. And over all these virtues put on love, which binds them all together in perfect unity."
Colossians 3: 12-13 NIV

You may wonder, "How can a God who can see all the decisions we've made and all of our thoughts, still love us as though we've done nothing wrong?" I know I blamed Him for everything and told Him that everything was His fault. I said many hurtful words. How could He still love me? Because that is who He is. He is actually the definition of LOVE. Take a minute and think of someone that you know absolutely loves you. For me, that person is my mom. There has never been anything I have ever done that would change her love for me. She knows about all the wrong things I have done. I have said some very hurtful things to her in the past, one of the biggest being that the husband she trusted and loved, had abused me. Yet today, she still chooses me and she still loves me. There were consequences for some of my actions and some sadness that came as a result of the actions of others, but her love never changed. It's the love of a mother. I now understand it even more that I have my two baby girls. There is literally nothing that could make me love them less. The only reason we have this kind of love is because God blessed us with it. I like to think that He also gave it to us so that we can better understand Him and His love for us.

"Or what man is there among you who, if his son asks for bread, will give him a stone? 10 Or if he asks for a fish, will he give him a serpent? 11 If you then, being evil, know how to give good gifts to your children, how much more will your Father who is in heaven give good things to those who ask Him! 12 Therefore, whatever you want men to do to you, do also to them, for this is the Law and the Prophets." Matthew 7: 9-12 NKJV

Take that love and times it by 1000, and that might be closer to His love for us. I know some of you did not have a mom or someone you were counting on, stand by your side. I am so sorry. But trust me, God will stand and is standing by your side. He will also provide an army of people that will help you and walk with you every step of the way. BUT now we know God's nature and that He is love and that he doesn't do anything that is not love, right? So, what is the only other option? Where is the evil coming from? Satan. In the same way that Heaven is so real, Hell is real too. And in the same way that there is an amazing God, there is a horrible, evil devil too. And he is a liar. But most importantly, you need to know that he is defeated.

"The thief comes except to steal, and to kill, and to destroy; I have come that they may have life, and that they may have it more abundantly. "I am the good shepherd. The good shepherd gives His life for the sheep." John 10:10-11 NKJV

Satan knows it's easy to blame God for things that He didn't do because God is just so good and He won't even defend Himself most of the time. However, Satan is the sneaky liar who keeps whispering in your ear, being a thief, stealing your peace, robbing you of your safety and security, taking your joy. Don't let this scare you because when you belong to God, Satan has no power over you, only what you give to him. WAIT, WHAT? Yes, read that again! You may say, "Satan has NO power? But then why is he so scary and evil?" For sure you don't want to play around with the evil side because the devil has been around for a long time and he knows how to work things in his favour. But he is like an imposter on an online dating site. He has a fake profile picture of a young, jacked, handsome guy with a very good job who became a millionaire by age 24. When you start talking to him, he seems great and so you choose to meet him in person. You arrange to do that in a public place. As you wait for him to arrive, you look hard and you think, "WAIT a second! Is that you, Bob?" The guy approaching you is a skinny, old, bald man with two teeth and a walking cane. He can't even speak properly. He's half blind because his glasses are broken, and because he has just lost all his money, he is now living on the streets! Totally super dramatic, yes, but it is an illustration to show you that satan likes to show off and pretend he is all that when, in reality, he is so weak that when you have God in you, you can literally step on him like an ant.

I remember that when I was little, I was so scared of my wall next to my bed. At night, I would hear a sound as though someone was scratching at my wall. I thought it was a ghost or something outside trying to kill me. Running, terrified and crying, I went for my mom. In a panic I said, "Mom there is something outside trying to kill me!"

She ran to my bedroom (we did live in Mexico at the time, so yes, she ran) and with a little smile said, "Alexia there is nothing to be afraid of. Come with me. There is always an explanation behind everything." Hiding behind my mom, outside we went and sure enough, she pointed to the palm tree that had been brushing up against my wall. "See Alexia! That big leaf has been brushing against the wall that your bed is next to. There is a lot of wind, so it is not a ghost or anyone trying to get you. It was all in your head, so go back to sleep." Then quickly I felt safe and kind of silly. I was able to fall asleep even with the same scratching sound. Had my mom never taken me outside to see the root of the problem, I would have still been terrified and unable to sleep. Something as simple as a leaf can become so big and so real and so scary in your life, yet it is just an insignificant leaf. That is the exact same way satan is. He plays with your mind, making himself look so big and scary when, with God inside you, he is only a leaf. God is a good God and He loves you so much. It is NOT in His nature to hurt you. It is the opposite actually! So, if you have surrendered your life to Jesus already, call it like it is and literally tell satan to be quiet and to go back where he came from! Everything that comes out of his mouth is a lie straight from hell, and hell is somewhere where even demons don't want to go!

Jesus asked him, saying, "What is your name?"
And he said, "Legion," because many demons had entered him. 31 And they begged Him that He would not command them to go out into the abyss. (Abyss is another word for Hell.)
Luke 8: 31 NKJV

Before I go on, I would also like to quickly say something about online dating. There are many people with very bad intentions using online dating. If you choose to do that, always meet a person in a very public place and even better, with a few friends. Do not send them pictures of yourself, especially vulnerable pictures. I know that there are people for whom online dating has worked. Personally, I am not advising that you do it. But if you are, just please use wisdom.

If you know anything about the Bible, the first book of the Bible that people like to quote when something bad is going on is the book of Job. They like to say, "Well like Job, God has allowed this to happen to me. It's just a test, I guess." If you don't know what I'm talking about when I say Job, it's a book in the Bible that tells the story about a man who was a great person and had a great life. He was wealthy, had a good family, and enjoyed a great relationship with God. But one day, terrible things began to happen. His children died and everything that he owned was destroyed! Even Job himself got sick to the point of death! If there was anybody who had had a bad day, it was him! The devil was out to destroy him and all he had! And God seemed to let him! But why? How can a loving God do that to his faithful, loving son?

God was the one who had called Job blameless and upright. God was the one who had blessed him so much that he was the greatest of all the men of the east. (Job 1) And it made the devil mad. He had wanted a "way in" to destroy him for a long time. The devil had set his heart against Job, to destroy him. And then one day, the devil came to God because Job had finally provided him with a way in, and open door, Fear. Job had fear in his heart for his children and would go every day to burn an offering for them hoping they would be good with God. (Job 1: 5) Therefore he had fear, and that is something that is not from God. It is the opposite of faith, and you cannot have both. Job chose to fear for his kids instead of believing what God had already told him: that his kids would be blessed. And God, because He will always stay true to His word, had to let Job have from what he had chosen. The devil now had the ability to touch Job's life and to bring the results of Job's choosing to fear for his kids instead of believing in God's ability to protect his kids. God will always honour what we choose, and the devil knows it. Everything was in the devil's hands where Job was concerned because Job had made choices that PUT it into his hands, and God had to honour what Job chose. Though Job had a hedge of protection around him that had been put there by a loving God, Job himself had provided the opening in that hedge with his fear, and that was all that satan needed. That's why satan could go to God and prove that he had a legal right to touch Job's life with terrible stuff.

Some things happen to us in our lives because we have "opened a door". But how can that door be closed? Am I doomed forever? NO! Not at all! That is another reason that Jesus came. He went to the Cross so that now you and I can easily ask God for forgiveness and we can repent of our choices that have let the devil have access into our lives, and the doors that we have opened can be easily shut! While you have been reading, if something has come to your mind that you have "opened a door" to the enemy (the devil) with, you can simply recognize it, repent of it, and break your agreement with it. If you belong to Jesus, that will close that door again. But remember, keep it shut!

An easy prayer for that is:

God, I have done _____
(And then name the thing: watching something I should not have, allowing unforgiveness, having hate, jealousy, whatever it is - name it) I confess it to You. I know it is wrong. I ask You to forgive me for it. And right now, I break all agreement with it, and I commit with Your help, not to be involved in that again. I break any "contracts" I could have

made with the devil by my involvement in that thing and I
sever any ties to it with the blood of Jesus Christ, and in the
name of Jesus. It is done.

That's how easy it is. Whatever door you have allowed to
be opened, can be shut that easily. But what if you were not the
one to open that door? Can that happen as well? Yes, it can. It is
something called a "generation curse". These are things that can
be passed down from generation to generation. It is similar to blue
eyes being passed down to you from your grandpa and your dad,
or your mom's amazing singing ability. You have inherited it. In a
similar way, generational curses can be passed down. For example,
your great-grandfather may have been an alcoholic and that then
passed down to your dad and now you struggle in that area. Or
perhaps none of your family members before you have been able
to graduate from post-secondary schooling. Those things can be a
result of a generation curse. But there is good news! It is so simple
to break off. In my case sexual abuse was a generation curse. It was
a sexual bondage that had passed down generationally to my dad.
So, we decided that was the end of that! We broke that generation
curse, and many more while we were at it!

Once you have given your life to Jesus, here is how you can break
them off so that you can be the END of that "yuck", and be the start
of a new generation, a generation of victors not victims, believers not
unbelievers, free not captive, and for the generations to come!

God, in the name of Your Son Jesus, I choose to break
off this generation curse (name it here). I choose to be a

new generation. I repent for being involved in it in any way. I break it off of me with the blood of Jesus Christ. And devil, you are not allowed to touch me or any of my future generations in this area any longer!

See how simple God makes it when you belong to Him? There is no 5-hour prayer to be set free! Why am I telling you all of this? I want you to see that God is a good God. I want you to see the things that can go on behind the scenes that can play into why things happen. I want you to see that it's the devil that wants to steal from you, kill, and destroy you. Once I understood all of this, I saw that it was not God who had just allowed things to happen to me. He was actually fighting for me and had kept me alive! He had directed me to find Him so that I could get complete victory and return to His perfect plan for my life. Has what I've gone through made me a different person? Yes, yes it has! It has made me more compassionate and happier. I enjoy life more, and it is easy for me to forgive people because nothing anyone has done to me has been worse than what my dad did, or has made it harder to forgive than my dad. But I have forgiven him!

God loves you, sister or brother! He loves you so much that He pointed you to this book! He loves you so much that He wants you to be happy with nothing holding you back! I promise that if you sit down and write out on a sheet of paper every day all the blessings you got that day, you will have a full page! How do I know? I did that for three years, and I have 5 journals full of His blessings! I encourage you to do it. It helped me to visualize His love even if I was having a bad day. It helped me to realize that He was with me in the little things while I was busy looking at the one bad thing that day. It will help you to see how God cares about every detail of your day. He is not too busy to hear you. On the contrary, He is waiting for you to talk to him! You are perfect and beautiful from the inside out because He made you! And if He didn't want you, He would never have created you. Know that He chose you and has BIG plans for you!

John 3:16 NKJV "For God so loved the world that He gave His one and only begotten Son, that whoever believes in Him shall not perish but have everlasting life."

1 John 4: 7-8 NKJV "Beloved, let us love one another, for love is of God; and everyone who loves who loves is born of God and knows God. He who does not love does not know God, for God is love."

Romans 8:31-32 NKJV "If God is for us, who can be against us? He who did not spare His own Son, but delivered Him up for us all, how shall He not with Him also freely give us all things?"

Romans 8:37-39 NKJV "Yet in all things we are more than conquerors through Him who loved us. For I am persuaded that neither death nor life, nor angels nor principalities nor powers, nor things present nor to come, nor height nor depth, nor any other created thing, shall be able to separate us from the love of God which is in Christ Jesus our Lord."

Lastly, if you still don't have Jesus in your life and you want to give your heart to Him today so that He can start to work in your life, pray this prayer. Pray that He would simply come and invade your life with His love! But make sure you are ready to make this decision and are not taking it lightly.

Salvation prayer

Lord Jesus, I believe you are truly the Son of God. I confess that I have sinned against you in thought, word, and deed. Please forgive all my wrongdoing and let me live in relationship with you from now on. I receive you are my personal Savior, accepting on my behalf the work you accomplished once and for all on the cross. Thank you for saving me. Help me to live a life that is pleasing to you.

If you just chose to accept Jesus as your personal Saviour, the one that died for your sins, I encourage you to find a Christian Church that will help and love you. Ask God to bring the right people into your life who will help you and not hold you back! Talk to your pastor and join church groups that are fitting for your age, and God will bring good friends to you to walk with you every step of the way! Church is where I have found my best of friends and a church family that will stick by you no matter what.

You did it, you finished reading the book! Now you have the steps to change your story and go from victim to victor. Know you are loved, I am praying for you, and I am your biggest fan!

IF HE DID IT FOR ME,
HE CAN DO IT FOR YOU!

Prayers

Salvation prayer:

Lord Jesus, I believe you are truly the Son of God. I confess that I have sinned against You in thought, word, and deed. Please forgive all my wrongdoing and let me live in relationship with You from now on. I receive You as my personal Saviour, accepting on my behalf the work You accomplished, once and for all, on the cross. Thank you for saving me. Help me to live a life that is pleasing to You.

Severing soul ties prayer:

In the name of Jesus, I sever all <u>ungodly</u> spirit, soul, and body ties with _____ (name the person). I take back to myself any part of me that was connected to him/her. I give back to him/her any part of him/her that was connected to me. I now sever with the Blood of Jesus all ungodly spirit, soul, and body ties with _____ (name the person again).

Breaking generational curses prayer:

God, in the name of Your Son Jesus, I choose to break off this generation curse (name it here). I choose to be a new generation. I repent for being involved in it in any way. I break it off of me with the blood of Jesus Christ. And devil, you are not allowed to touch me or any of my future generations in this area any longer!

Closing open doors to the devil prayer:

God, I have done _____ (And then name the thing: watching something I should not have, allowing unforgiveness, having hate, jealousy, whatever it is – name it) I confess it to You. I know it is wrong. I ask You to forgive me for it. And right now, I break all agreement with it, and I commit with Your help, not to be involved in that again. I break any "contracts" I could have made with the devil by my involvement in that thing and I sever any ties to it with the blood of Jesus Christ, and in the name of Jesus. It is done.

Forgiveness prayer:

I (name), choose to forgive (name) for (say what the person(s) did) today. I choose to live in freedom and let go of this hurt. God, I pray for Your strength and for Your grace. Thank you, Lord, that I can trust in Your promises. It is finished. It is paid for and given to me freely by the blood of Jesus Christ. Amen.

Daily "medicine" or "face cream":

"God loves you, (add your name here). I am loved in Heaven and I am loved on the earth. I am beautiful for I have been made in the image and likeness of God. I am fearfully and wonderfully made. God adores me. I am His treasure. I do not need a man (or woman, if you are a male reader) to complete me. I am complete in Jesus. I am God's daughter/son and He delights in me. I am an heir of God and a

joint-heir with Jesus, I am worth SO MUCH! I can do anything, I have gifts, talents and abilities given to me by God and there is nothing I cannot do. Jesus loves me, and God loves me as much as He loves His own son Jesus. Because of that truth, I am worth the very best. I love the Lord my God with ALL my heart, with ALL my soul, with ALL my mind, and with ALL my strength. I love others as I love myself, but I do not need other people to complete me. Jesus does that for me, I am complete and content in Him."

My Suggestions

Some teachings that have helped me live victoriously, or I mentioned in the book are:

1. Lisa Bevere   "Kiss the Girls and Made Them Cry" (book & workbook)
2. Lisa Bevere   "Purity Is Power" (CD teaching)
3. Lisa Bevere   "Without Rival (book)
4. John Bevere   "Porn Free" (book or other)
5. Jesse Duplantis   "What in Hell Do You Want" (DVD teaching)

Songs that encourage me:

1. Kari Jobe   "I Am Not Alone"
2. Kari Jobe   "The More I Seek You"
3. Britt Nicole   "All this time"
4. Jonathan and Melissa Helser   "No longer Slaves"
5. King and Country   "Priceless"
6. Kristene Dimarco   "I Am No Victim"
7. Lauren Daigle   "You Say"
8. Lauren Daigle   "Rescue"

Printed in the United States
By Bookmasters